I MAY OR MAY NOT LOVE YOU

DAVID M. PERKINS

ICE CUBE PRESS   LLC
NORTH LIBERTY IOWA - USA

I May or May Not Love You

Copyright © 2020 David M. Perkins
First Edition

ISBN 9781948509152

Library of Congress Control Number:2019954882

Ice Cube Press, LLC (Est. 1991)
North Liberty, Iowa 52317 USA
www.icecubepress.com | steve@icecubepress.com
Follow on Facebook or Twitter

The paper used in this publication meets the minimum
requirements of the American National Standard
for Information Sciences—Permanence of Paper for
Printed Library Materials, ANSI Z39.48-1992.

Manufactured in USA

Credits: "I Should Have No Doubts," First Prize Ann Woodbury
Hafen Poetry Award; "The Goblins'll Get You" originally
published in *High Plains Literary Review*; "Outliving the
Rhyme," originally published in *Grasshopper: A New Journal
of Poetry*; "The Last Days of Sebastian Melmoth," originally
published in *The Bloomsbury Review*/republished in *When
the Bluebird Sings: An Oscar Wilde Journal*; "Epilogue to
a Moral Fable," originally published in *Christopher Street
Magazine*; "Dark Ages" originally published in *The Chariton
Review*; "Sentiment for a City," originally published in
76 Centennial Stories; "Sirius, Andromeda, Betelgeuse,"
originally published in *Grasshopper: A New Journal
of Poetry*; "Schadenfreude," originally published in *The
Chariton Review*; "Weather Whether," originally published in
*Ság
a: A Poetry Journal*.

"We paint from within outward—if we force our vision on the world it calls us great painters; if we don't it ignores us; but we are the same. We don't attach any meaning to greatness or smallness. What happens to our work afterward is unimportant; we have got all we could out of it while we were doing it."
— W. Somerset Maugham

TABLE OF CONTENTS

Illustrations:

To catch a poem in
midair, spiral off with
it, tension never bent
back in—that's the thing.
Yes, and damn cleancut,
annihilate quite, without
rancor or relief...

—William Tillson, from *Walden Invaded*

DEDICATION

For These

*For those who had other better things to do
and couldn't wait until today, I miss you:
Mom, who taught me poems are laugh out
loud, and to Jeff and Val who found their
brother odd, and to Dick and Glenda who
couldn't take it anymore; and Phil and Kerry,
Warren and James, Diana and Tami, taken
because not enough of us cared: I miss you,
this is the best I can do, these are for you.*

*But above all, to the only poem who matters,
to my son, Daysun (sorry, honey, if I had been
better, this would have been money), who never
faltered, forever loves, and unfailingly forgave.*

PREFACE: An Apologia

Tell all the Truth but tell it slant—
Success in Circuit lies
—Emily Dickinson

I have read the great poets for umpty-odd years. I started at age six with *Favorite Poems Old and New: Selected for Boys and Girls* by Helen Ferris (still have my copy and still read in it), and went on to attend all the various "Schools of," but I was never matriculated in any particular one—I listened however, paid attention—there's always something to be learned (if one is wise enough to stay out of the weeds).

From Auden to Cummings to Eliot, from Ashbery to Basho to Millay, from Frost to Swenson to Plath, from Donne to Ginsberg to Anonymous, from Dickinson to Dame Edith Sitwell to Ogden Nash, I sit at their feet and honor every word. I know what makes a poem good, what shapes they should take, and how they should sound. Those and others have left so much treasure strewn around, it would be criminal not to lift some of it, and I have been a greedy if not very stealthy thief.

But the poems here, if indeed that's what they are, have an issue with obedience. They breezed in with a phrase or a line and flew ahead of me galloping; banging consonants together and rolling vowels like bowling balls down the hall. They flung assonance and alliteration around like confetti, they contrapuntally chimed rhymes off-key and off-kilter, and it was all I could do to galumph along behind them trying to make order and sense out of it before they disappeared to wherever it is they go when they finished making a mess of my mind. Tidying up took forever.

I'm fond of them because they're variously merrily depressed and somberly absurd, and they all came at me with this irritatingly distracting joy; my mortal clumsiness and cluelessness made them laugh; they sent me back to poets who did it better, and occupied hours when I should have been doing something useful and productive. If you like them, good; if you don't, take it up with the errant, vexatious visitors who danced through my door and never bothered to knock. Thing is, nobody can really tell you what poems are or ought to be, and no one should try to tell you, especially not me. I used it on the cover because I don't know what else to call them and to gesture vaguely in the direction of something familiar. If I did it right, you'll see as much of you in them as me.

I've rarely tried to find them a home other than my own, tucked some in this box, stuck some in that file, folded them to mark where I stopped reading between the pages of another book, rarely shared them with anyone who might be unkind, and packed them up to cross the country with me a half-dozen times. They're only here because some kind souls heard them and said *For God's sake, let them have some air!* So here they are—good luck to them, and good luck to you.

Oh, do not ask, "What is it?"
Let us go and make our visit.
— T.S. Eliot

I Should Have No Doubts

There should be no shame in telling
what I see.
I should have no shouting doubts
crowding my vision.
I am a first of May, wary
of swinging from branches,
though falling to the lawn
is not frightful.

Should I admit to the tickling
of toadish temptations
in a false garden?
I should say I can see
the world as worm-weary
as the birds do
and see it as it was,
as the birds do
that have flown again
from Florida to flutter
in the street gutters where there
were only weeds once.

I should say how the sun feels
when it falls into the valley
of the clock.
And how it looks, steaming the
east wall of houses
and falling into the dark and dew-cold
shadows of their west walls
leaning toward evening like
airless moons
in the frozen explosions of space.

I should tell how bread crumbs look,
spread among the rapes of morning papers,

and see, the cars are crowding,
blue breath banners streaming,
to pay and lay allegiance
at the city's crown of towers.
And at twenty-three, I can see
the afternoon sun throw a ripped ray
into committee rooms and lean against
old maid curtains and slither
down the walls of clocks.

At evening I will say how I can see the buildings
lean mascara-caked into midnights lit with
red and yellow stars
and wrapped in orange smoke.

Where I Wonder

So might it have gone
had I done one
small thing different.
Had I said
no
not now or
yes, please.

Had I gone,
had I stayed at home,
if I had kissed this one
and not that one.
Had I decided to miss
that train and took
a later one.

If I had not had one
drink more or had
I not turned that one down.
Had I,
where those two roads
diverged, decided
to turn back instead
and start all over again
from where I knew I was
and not gone down either
not caring where
they were leading.

Had I foregone that seemingly
glittering opportunity
where the golden ring
hung temptingly from
Fortune's finger and
passed on to see what other

treasure might yet be
uncovered.

Had I let the fine bones
of Paris seduce me,
had I met you halfway,
had I held you tighter,
had I let you drift away,
had I said something like
maybe—
where, then, I wonder,
would we be?

Makings

Living in the city I hear
so many voices outside
so many lives in passing
conversations by my door.

As others like the sound
of streams or breezes
in reverberation among
the rocks or trees

I like these:
disembodied words
that scratch against the glass,
that lilt or roar and swear

or lyrically slur
late night stories
or stumbling songs to tell
me they are there.

This small island
with its beach abreast
the flow and its raucous will
adrift my window.

We Still Quietly Suppose

We set about our days
with purpose: these things
to do, and those that
should have been done
yesterday (or days before),
and slot them into our
allotment of hours from
covers-off to bed-down,
from sun-east to sun-west
and then some.

Among them, almost gone
unnoticed, like sparrows
bundled in brown branches,
like the whoosh of cars
outside our window, among
the windings of our mind
bent over our check-list
of chores, small wishes appear
and dot our thoughts like end-
stops at the tail of sentences.

We make them, then move on.
We may not preface them
with "I wish," but still made:
small negligible ones or larger
that fit into a momentary day-
dream of how things could
be better—if. After all these
long ungratified years of error
and disappointment, like children
we still quietly suppose in magic
it seems.

Doing what we need to do to get
through our mostly useful if,
to be honest, commonplace days,
the wizard within sets aside the
practical for the second it takes
to flash an exceptional alternative
to what is, or will be, and sends it
blazing through the ordered Universe
for its thoughtful consideration.

Disconcerting Things
(for Bruce Joshua Miller)

If we were to find a way
out of this mess,
what a relief it would be—
like winning the lottery.

Even the best of dreams
are full of disconcerting things:
the way your house can be
an entirely different place
for instance, or your friends
all someone else.

Still, the lure of having everything
organized, the overwhelming complications
whittled to a manageable size
is tempting—even, perhaps,
dealing with the possibility
of no surprise at all for a while
would be comforting.

It's the unknown hiding with a lead pipe
down the alleys of our days that
gets us, that catches us unarmed
and embarrassed in the middle
of our waking and naked
in our hope.

By the Light

The blind moon trails
her pale fingers of light
across the gray face
of the Earth, feeling for
change—here, another
acre of rainforest gone
to ash and plow, there
a fresh scar where a
highway will be, here
a development where the
tassels of corn-stalks once
waved silkily, and there,
a fresh mound of ground
where an aging admirer
once stood and gazed
at her wan countenance
and loved her waning
and her waxing ways.

Every cloud-free night an
altered Earth presents its
face to the soft fingertips of
moonlight, tracing change,
keeping her counsel, knowing
it's only a matter of time.

Some Kind of Ars Poetica

This is a poem
about poems
about poems
(which always occur
when the muse is away).
Poems about poems
tell us,
in the best possible poetical way,
that poems about poems
are poems that tell us
about poems
in the best possible poetical way.

This is a poem
about poems
about poems
however,
and really has nothing to say.

Philadelphia/Red Cloud
(for Kathleen Cain)

My friend here opts for openness—
a prairie that tests
the ability of the eye to reach
that single tree
where tired with distance
the horizon rests.

And she knows its name
as well as she knows
that small brown fleck in the sky
is a hawk
and how each of the grasses
tosses the sounds of the wind along.

She's come to the city
to visit me.
I offer her the civilized smells
of the street
and eerie stare of skyscrapers' eyes
at night and people from the edge
of life who talk to no one there
and dark clattering rides
through municipal burrows
to alien meals.

In the evening
narrowed by wine
over the music
while the city snaps at the door
we bend like witches over a cauldron
and give each other
our captured gifts.

The Goblins'll Get You

Ghosts.
My mother's mother's ghost
on the side of the highway
scuffing her spectral shoes
in the dirt on her dry way
to a bar. My mother's father's
ghost looks for a light
for his long unlit cigar.
My father's mother's ghost
tries to suck air
through from another dimension.
My mother's ghost on a
suburban hill, angry at
strangers in her house.
My best friend's ghost
sits in a car, the gray
barrel of a shotgun
between his spook-white
teeth, listening to his
demons speak. My sister's
ghost, lost in a valley
in Nepal, fades into
Annapurna's shade, looking
for Americans, for family.
They discovered how
to flee, and my ghost
strides with something
called purpose down
34th Street, with something
to say, something to say to each.

I Would, For You

Is it safe here, now,
do you suppose?

These last seconds were.

And there, another few have flown
and nothing untoward
occurred.

Where did I put
that word last?

Would it fit best here
now that so much time has elapsed?

Love.

There it sits and seems
to fit fine
in the context.

If I stare at it
sometimes it seems to glow.

If only it were within my power
to fan that flowering ember

I would,
for you,
and set this page ablaze.

Listen to the Night
(for Daysun, Age 6)

The sheets of days
are sliding between us accumulating changes
we will never have the time to share.

Sleep
in the arms of innocence and night
miles away and miles deep
in dreams in another man's home
while he holds your mother
and whispers in the dark
and keeps her warm.

My talk will not disturb them
though you frown and sigh
and pull your pillow to your ear.
I will speak quietly in the vowels
of the moon's voice round
and silver.

What do you do with your foreign life?
Are you free to cross the fields?
Do you hide your peas in the cuff of your pants?
When you wonder where the sun goes,
do they tell you true (or try to fool you
as I might do with a monstrous purple lie)?

I'm sorry.
Did I speak too loud?
Maybe our messenger the moon has just
gone behind a cloud, but I could swear
I heard some voice
reply.

Time makes distance farther
and out of my control you grow
to the dictates of different weather.
When the days we have together
winnow, then cease—
when the daylight of life

intervenes between choices and dreams
and you have what seems to be all
of forever before you—if you feel you are somewhere
love cannot reach, then

listen to the night
and for the lullabies the moon sings.

None of Us
(for SJJ)

We are none of us someone
else, and the specters who stalk
us, sorrow or strife or something
other, all have a different face—
resembling ours of course so we
might recognize them, but awry
enough to throw their shadow
alarmingly across our day.

Sometimes others see them and
know we're being haunted in
an arcane way and duck their
heads to see if under the cowl
they might catch our eyes and
pull the one they know out from
under the pall that's fallen there.

And then others misconstrue
and when even just a gentle word
would do, turn away or say, *this
won't do, I don't see it that way,*
or imply the fault is in us, not
the ignis fatuus that has oozed
its way into the mechanisms of
our complicated singularity.

Some have said that Plato, who saw
us better than we see ourselves once
wisely advised, *Be kind, for everyone
you meet is fighting a hard battle.*
We are none of us someone
else, and the specters who stalk
us, sorrow or strife or something
other, all have a different face.

The Yellow Wood
Une chanson d'amour

I do not want to lead you astray. I do not want
you to go unaccompanied through the yellow
wood. I do not want to lie to you and will not.

I do not want to make it difficult for you; I do
not want to make it complicated. I do not want
you to feel uneasy, as though I cannot be trusted

with your feelings. I do not want the way to be
too hard, but worth the effort. I certainly do not
want you to get the perception that I think I am

somehow smarter than you because I am not.
I do not want to confuse you with riddles and
symbols that you would have to be me to know.

I want it to be plain and clear so that you can see
all the way through the water to the round pebbles
underneath the sparkling stream light. I do not

want the clouds interfering with your ability to see
beyond the atmosphere into the deep night where
stars are born and die in billions of years gone by.

I want you to step easily into me and feel comfortable
and calm, though storms may be going on, and
touch the reachable in ways your mind will recount

in perfect detail days and ages later. I do not want
you to be afraid or puzzled or feel as though you
may have been fooled. I want you to separate

yourself from your skin and step out into the air
and realize that there is someone there to catch
you. I want to travel with you as far as you will go.

A Small Melody

It's only a small melody
that haunts me, appearing
out of the silence that too
often surrounds me. It may
rise humming or whistle
in when my mind is other-
wise occupied, when I am
engaged in those mundane
things that roadblock our
days that must always be
attended to to move ahead.

From a suite or symphony
(I never remember which
until I meet it again in
context), but it has sealed
itself somehow into my
mind, become inextricably
bound with the whole of
myself, like atoms that
bond with others it has
become another entity
inside, an element, with-
out which I would not
be wholly me it seems.

I did not choose this
companion, it chose me
and took up residency
moving in seemingly
to stay, but it could be
worse, at least it's not
a commercial jingle
jangling its *buy! buy!*
at me, its meaning is

none other than to be.
And so am I, and so
I welcome it in, and
carry it carefully with
me as I would the love
of a life-long friend.

Some Are Too Shy to Travel There

Although they often may not mean to
(some do), critics might shame us into
believing we should believe as they do,
arguing their thoughts and arguments,
their reasons and their wherefores well,
and telling us to be our best we should
look through their own window wisely
and we will see things as they see them.

We should respect them, they have gone
into the field, plowing, seeding, cultivating
and bringing unsung buds to flower where
there were only weeds once. They have a
worthwhile power. We need them; further
where would we be without that husbandry?
I will not dismiss either their insightful hits
or damning misses, they mostly mean well.

I'm thinking this as I finish a long day of
labor, and needing to unwind, I turn to a
favorite of mine, Tchaikovsky, to take me
otherwhere for a time, and give audience to
Manfred, the outlier among his otherwise
numbered symphonies, often overlooked,
shamefully evaded in our modern concert
halls, and rise on the tide of his melodies.

Critics have not been as kind as they might
to Pyotr Ilyich, scoffing at his "heart on his
sleeve," his sorrow sown among the strings,
the parading of his fantasies, his sentiments
laid plain for all to see. Some, it would seem
are too shy to travel there, into candor and
rawness of the heart. The second movement,
then, the Scherzo, flew in on a flutter of flutes.

The Alpine Fairy arrives in a rainbow, on high
strings and harp, a rainbow flung from the spray
of an alluvion waterfall—and then the tears start.
After a long and arduous day, I have been taken
far away into hearing themes we dare not say,
into enchantment, bewitchment, and wizardry.
Critics, there are ways beyond words to travel—
it was magic today that made the world unravel.

On Listening to Tchaikovsky's
Autumn Song: October, Op. 37a.

There is a melody here in October
more melancholy than other airs
when night begins to ink its way
earlier into the daylight hours and
days diminish downward toward
the polar crevasse of the year.

The morning glories still warm
themselves against the south
wall of the house and bay out
their blues for wayward wasps
and bees—but ice whispers its
chill warnings into their ears.

The leaves feel the southerly
drag of the sun drawing its
rays away and they seep their
green back deep into the trees
leaving the brittle, crisp reds
and gold of their bones behind.

October soothes the summer
into its annual slumber, and
somberly prepares its wardrobe
for the winter widow's weeds
that solemnly, inevitably follow.
Linger here but for moments only

and listen: the languid melody
of October as the days unfold.

Outliving the Rhyme
(for Richard Joseph Peake, 1946-1975)

Words are such cold things—
if I could pump blood
into the word
hug
I would.
If you could press
your mouth to the word
lips
as they wait here
on this page
and taste them
then I would have succeeded
somewhat.
If
love
could be spelled
with the sound of my voice
even when you were away
I could say it to you
and you would be reminded.
If I could put
all
of myself here
how convenient it would be—
I could be folded
and put in your pocket.
I could be with you always.
I could be something warm
you could have carried to your grave.

The Songs of Mothers

There are times I wish to say
instead:
only the whisper of words,
long calm-voweled sentences that lullabies use,
the soothing of cooing, crooning
sounds that say nothing.
Those that sigh in the evening
when the moonrise is a high round O
in the sky, a silver-circled mirror
reflecting the songs of mothers who know
the hour is safe, their babies asleep,
and feel too tender to leave them to solitary
or unaccompanied dreams.

After the Tone

Once again I've gone
to voicemail.
That friendly guard that
takes the voice of we unseen
and puts it in a place safe
for you to get to when
you have the time and wish to,
to tell you of the drama accumulated
while you were otherwise
indisposed.

This is me.
Not much to relate, really,
the train was late—oh
and how did your visit with
what's-his-name go? Outside
the weather has turned cold and
different colored leaves like supplicants
blow against my door as if attracted to
some sanctuary they might find within.
Nothing more. When you can,
give me a call.

Leave me a message if I'm not
near enough to answer.

As Long as All Goes Well
(for DBW)

Of course I know that you love another
(I would too, if I could help myself)—
I'm smitten, not a fool—but I'll linger
here nevertheless in your periphery
in case you ever need me and keep
tabs on the public self you share and
never intrude as long as all goes well.

Loving you is no burden to me and
shouldn't be for you either, I mean
love is one of those things you can't
control, like the weather or your
mood when you haven't slept well.

Love is a helium-filled balloon and
at the same time the rock it's tethered
to, and the tension that holds the two
together—both gravity and lighter
by far than air. It's all that isn't and
all there is, all there was and all that
could ever be. To dismiss it is to
refuse to breathe, so go ahead with
your life far away from my words
or reach, and inhale deeply, my dear,
forever is the sweetest burden to bear.

Here Today, Wheresoever Tomorrow

Chop.
And everything that could be
severed was—
left behind.
The baggage past
as neatly uncoupled
as if it were a train car
unpinned and left to drift slowly
to a halt
somewhere on the perspective behind me.

There's only so much one can miss,
after all, change will come
in and rearrange the now in any case
like some ruthless, remodeling crew
determined to make it new,
make it new,
no matter what.

I've saved a few
chloroformed moments—
some lovely, if dead ones—
pinned on a word or two
here and there and pressed
between pages.

The Last Days of Sebastian Melmoth*

The sun down this narrow Paris street creeps
and squares a small field of large
magenta blooms on the wall
in this room.
These blossoms do not green
or grow, but fade in the daily path
under the golden steps the sun takes
travelling the wall
to finally fall on this table
where no writing but begging will be done.
Even the friendship my pen once held for me
has gone and the afternoon
rises on dust in the shaft of sun
that shines and illuminates the fading blooms
where I, alone, room—
waiting patiently for the evening post,
for the last slipper of sun
to leave the last petal,
desert the plain table
and disappear into the dusk, ah,
where absinthe and lust
wait for me down the narrow Paris streets
in the arms and eyes
of warm brown boys
whose arrows of love
martyr me.

[*Sebastian Melmoth was the name
Oscar Wilde assumed in exile after
being released from Reading Gaol.]

Epilogue to a Moral Fable

Dorothy lived there
for another year or so
and then her aunt,
followed by her uncle within three months
died, the tornado
had wrecked the farm anyway.
The hired hands were scattered
and Dorothy was sent to stay
with relatives even farther away
in the city where she could not keep her dog.
She was regarded as strange
and stand-offish,
given to flights of fancy.
But that was attributed to being
so long without family or friends.
Soon she was ready to attend the university.
It was there she learned,
much to her dismay,
she could not have a relationship
with any of the men
who understood her vision.
And, indeed, it soon became weeks
when she would not think
of where she had been
or what she had seen.

She is seventy-six now
and living in a nursing home
on her teacher's pension.
Some of her old students still
come to call
and listen very intently
when she begins to "carry on"
as her nurses call it—
and even then

some of them
will hang about the door
when she talks of going home again.

A Basket of Goodies

I had never seen
a naked man before.
I had no idea they could be
so hairy or make such
ugly grunting sounds.
What could you expect
a child to think?
He looked like a wolf to me.
I don't know when grandma died.
Hidden in her closet it seemed to go on forever.
All I remember is that her blood
seemed so much redder than
my riding coat, and my mother,
later, holding me so tight I was afraid I'd faint,
crying over my shoulder,
Animal! Animal!

Beauty and the Bargain

Oh, ho—he was fair!
More than fair.
He gave away his secret
so she could spare herself with gold.
I don't suppose we need to mention
what that transaction makes her,
no matter what her title now,
no matter how desperate then she seemed.
He even built a loophole in
(being too sure of himself
in this instance was his greatest sin).
But, surely, the need for love
ran as strong through his short, contorted
self as anyone?
Even, lonely as he was,
he might want to be a parent too?
Perhaps he could admire beauty more,
being such a stranger to her?
That which is beyond our crippled reach
only makes it seem that much more sweet.
Is it any wonder then, for once,
he rejoiced in his name as gnarled
as his face? Is it any wonder
he sang its rattling syllables and rolled
its vowels around in the forest air?
I suppose there can be a moral
where morality is concerned.
This, at the very least, can be learned from
Rumpelstiltskin:
Never bargain with a whore.

O My Fur and Whiskers!

At first, of course, no one believed her
any more than they would have believed the cat.
And nothing would have been whispered
if she had known enough
to keep her experiences to herself.
But, no—she insisted
on telling all the girls
upon returning to school and
in some cases, showing them
all she had learned on Mr. Dodgson's knee.
The Queen would certainly not
have believed it to say the least,
nor would she have been amused
had she known.
We know by the photographs
that Alice was a lissome thing,
and knowing now what we know
of Lolita, could we wonder just who it was
who fell down the rabbit hole that day?

Given a Life

Stitching the body together with fresh parts,
the doctor knew how vein fit to vein, muscle
to muscle, bone to bone, the medical arts
entirely at his command. He wrestled gristle

and ligaments into place and finding a fresh
brain still capable of fire, electrically stitching
synapse to synapse through the wired flesh,
making our monster at midnight, the witching

hour, by switching on the power and raising
the corpse to the top of the tower, he borrowed
lightning to bring him to life. On realizing
what he had done, he hauled the harrowed

body down and called him son. Across town
the misshapen crookback swung to his deaf
duties, clanging the bell clappers up and down
summoning with bangs and bongs he himself

could not hear, the faithful to prayer, bringing
sinners to their knees, the devout to confession
and Mass. His soundless, matin morning ringing
his contribution to redemption and to the broken

who could not bear to look upon his ghastly face
or shape. And the Fathers called him as everyone,
son. Not far from that stained-glass sacred space,
deep among other catacombs, burrows, and stone,

the phantom played his wild music, alone, alongside
the spiders, in the dank mold and gloom, improvising
cavernous hymns; hiding, denying the hideous sight
and reflection of his acid-seared face—played amazing

toccatas that raged of freedom and daylight, dawn
and spring, sang of children and breezes, deliverance,
and the look of enduring love that will never come.
He will never have a son. These are our own cousins

who had no opportunity to live, though given a life.
We bore them in the rank roiled confines of our mind
and made them eternal, our dread their prime midwife,
evermore trembling—afraid of our own kindred kind.

Distaff

The whole depressing mess of it was a chauvinist
conspiracy from its very genesis and remains so to
this day! I don't even have a *name*, for God's sake—

a major player in this shameful tale and I am eternally,
always, and only to be known as someone's wife?
Not, my friend, the greatest lot in life—or in history.

As far as I'm concerned, they are all imbeciles. Too
much fascination with, excuse me, their penises,
always wanting to brandish them about at the most

inopportune times. At least when they were hooded
you knew you were to be left alone for a while
and excuse me, I'm sorry, but that was yet another

incredibly dumb thing to do—*Oooh, God wants
us to*, they said, hacking at them with flints. Well,
fine, God didn't have to put up with all their daily

whining until they stopped hurting, didn't have
to bathe the pitiful things with herbs and spices
to help them heal. (At least they stayed out of trouble

for a while.) And always with the moving, moving.
There's not enough land for the two of us! Oy!—
and the squabbling? We were the ones to do the work

when they finally decided who would head north and
who south. Then the thing with the King, and then we
were saved with all the belongings and "goods." I swear.

Ah, yes—how did I become famous without a name?
I'm coming to it. All this has to be understood before
you can comprehend why I did what I did. Then it will

begin to make sense. After all the wandering, we finally
settled in the city and began to live fairly comfortably
for a change and I was glad to get him out of the house.

He spent his time hanging out with his cronies at the gate settling all the problems of the world no doubt and mentally undressing every woman who came in or out or wandered by

and drinking of course. That's what men do best together: drink themselves dizzy and metaphorically compare peckers. You can have them—nothing in the world is worth all that trouble.

Then he took to inviting strangers home. Glad-handing them at the gate, crocked, saying *Mi casa es su casa!* and bringing them home where (guess who?) was supposed to feed the useless lot.

He always called it *Hospitality!* Which I believe in and which any civilized person ought to—but all the time? Couldn't some of his fellow wastrel lay-abouts slop a trough sometime?

No, it always came down to us three, my daughters and me, to bake the bread, make the beds, and be welcoming, gracious, patient—while they thanked him for his generosity! The lot

of a wife is, let's be honest, a thankless one. When he brought home a bevy of stunning strangers is when the trouble began. I suppose I would have found it hard to say no myself when

I saw them arrive at the gate all resplendent and dressed to the nines. At least this was a compelling entourage, quite dazzled the eyes of everyone in town as he brought them

the long way home. But somehow the night went terribly awry. I admit I joined too much in the wine and what happened all became somewhat of a blur. I remember

the banging and the voices at the door, everyone wanting in, the insisting that these men had something more to share than their company—I have no idea how these things begin.

And then, for reasons I will never understand—to protect his *reputation for hospitality*, he said—the drunken sod offered our daughters instead! So, how would you react? What would

you have said? The man had obviously lost his head. And I had
to throw myself in front of the door to keep him in and the mob
out and our guests sat there like something carved in marble

and let him! Then they all conferred as if I were not in the room
mind you and he headed out—finally!—to get our daughters'
husbands-to-be (I thought, foolish me, for our protection) and

somehow I ended up packing again and we were running through
earthquake underfoot and through falling fire and found ourselves
fleeing for the hills. And then, *Don't look back! Don't look back!*

was all he said and kept on saying until finally I snapped.
I had had it with him and the trouble he was always getting
us into and having to leave the best home we had ever owned,

and all the miseries he had put us through and I stopped,
addressed the back of his balding head and said, *Fuck you, Lot!
I'm not going anywhere anymore with you!* and started back.

And do not try to tell me the incest began only *after* I was gone.

Dark Ages

Perched on a tall wooden stool I could
have been a monk with penmanship
trained to make such exquisite marks
on permanent parchment they would
linger forever, making their way to
museums and kept locked in the Rare
Book Room of libraries to be handled
only by experts and scholars with
clean white gloves.

Not even my own words but the
words of other men, illuminating
the text with colorful care,
my writing could have lasted
the ages—rather than these
all-too ragged unread things,
my own unkempt ideas in my
almost illegible hand. Even I
sometimes don't know what
I thought I meant and have to
invent another way of getting
through, like driving to a place
you've been to once and you faintly,
you think, know the way there.

It would not have been bad, at all,
that safe, undoubtedly short life
no decisions on what to wear,
menu planned, food provided,
prayers memorized so perfectly
that one could almost sleep through
them and then on to the pen, the
copying, even "begat" after "begat"
a way to fill up the day until
the light got too dim. Even if

no one believes anymore, they
would admire my words and how
they carved their ways through
my silent, chaste, and obedient days.

And no one would know how often
I stole a glance now and then at the
profile of the monk beside me, how
I memorized him as well, his head
bent over his pen and book, copying
carefully, and the thoughts I would
not bring to confession. Though we
were of course taught not to think
of our work with pride, I would—
particularly proud of how the letters,
the ink, shaped in elegant calligraphy,
ribbons of them running across and
then down beautifully, filling the page.

It would be better than this less than
inspired picking at my brain to bring
up an untidy tidbit or two to plunk on
this mass-produced paper, guessing,
knowing that no one will ever go to
the museum or library to don a pair
of clean white gloves to take a look
at this frivolous mess, this frittered life,
these words pinned unintelligible to
whatever remnant comes to hand. I
envy the monks who had God's words
at their fingertips and His blessing
on their efforts, knowing they would
be kept, even for heretics, unbelievers,
even though the monk did think things
he would never bring to confession.

If You're Dissatisfied with Your Lot

You know what I think? Caesar said,
swinging a be-sandaled foot and spitting
out an olive pit at an attendant slave,
*Life is too short to be powerless, but
power is such a heavy burden to bear,
I should know. Oh, it has its rewards—
no question there—but so much is
expected of one. Wherever something
of import appears, there you must be
as well, with all your senses wary of
treachery, not just from suspected
enemies, but friends and even family.*

He sighed and shifted his cloak to cover
his knees. *Gifts only go so far—even
those given to the gods and that's a
lot of expense for no guarantee of
return—my treasury is always running
low and everyone expects something
from me and it must be measured out
just so. Envy rises green among the
gods as easily as among my subjects,
you know. I could call my guards and
have your head spiked at an intersection
any time I wished and the gods could
have me as easily disenthroned and
exiled, or disemboweled and dead—
like that.* He languidly waved his hand.

*I would suggest you read your Plutarch
if you're dissatisfied with your lot. I have.
Good common sense is worth more than
any gold I could hand over to you for
your plans. I'm not an endless fount of
riches and simply can't grant everyone's*

wishes. Much as that might make me
popular it would also make me poor,
and I suspect that people expect more
from their Emperor than to wander
around in rags and serve inadequate
meals, lean gruel, and moldy bread.
So I'm sorry I must deny your request
for now. As I said, Plutarch—if you're
seeking peace of mind—has much more
to offer, much more than Caesar can.

Otherwhere

I would otherwise stop to say Goodbye,
but I'm in a hurry to Otherwhere.
Oh the Goddesses, how time does fly.

I meant to thank you for times gone by,
for the lift you gave me out of despair.
I would otherwise stop to say Goodbye,

but I can't wait—because the tide is high
and the songs of the Sirens are in the air.
Oh the Goddesses, how time does fly.

I must be off, there is a cloudless sky
and all the augurs warn I must beware,
I would otherwise stop to say Goodbye.

I would tell you but you mustn't ask why,
I have no choices, and none of it's fair.
Oh the Goddesses, how time does fly.

Please don't be angry, please let me by—
their cries are calling me from Otherwhere—
I would otherwise stop to say Goodbye.
Oh the Goddesses! How time does fly.

Boreas' Lament

It wasn't our plan
to cause anyone any harm.
But he had treated us shabbily.
Fickle and feckless with his love,
he was. His promises and sighs
in the night (dear sounds to us both)
made us believe the world
would always be spring and we
could control the weather.
He allowed us to caress his face
(his beautiful face!) and ruffle
his hair and dry his skin
after his swim—
but we weren't enough for him.
He had his sights set
on another.

Still, we only meant
to frighten him, to remind him
of our power and when
Zephyrus, who has never known
his own strength, altered the toss and delivered
(we forgot!) the mortal blow,
he died in someone else's arms.
Which is why, in summer, you will hear a sigh
when through the hyacinths we go.

[According to the legend, Hyacinthus was a beautiful
mortal loved by Apollo. Boreas and Zephyrus, gods
of the winds, also loved him and were jealous of the
love between Apollo and Hyacinthus. They caused
the discus being tossed between the two to strike
Hyacinthus in the forehead killing him. The hyacinth
flower sprang out of the blood from his wound.]

God Takes

An angel or an eagle—
the unkind say
a hawk—
dropped down and hooked
and hauled him away.

I had picked flowers,
violet, to match his eyes
when as I climbed I saw
a dark split in the sky that grew
descending black wings wide.
Time only for his name, I cried—
he turned—
his smile forever
frozen as if he had kissed
my mind, and then the talons
and the awful wrap of feathers—

gone—and the rock on
which he stood was stripped of life,
my life, my Ganymedes! gone.
The flowers wilting
at my feet in the sun.

Paccius to Plutarch: Greetings!

Thank you for your thoughts—
but don't you think too much
common sense is frightening
to most? You and I are old enough

to see what sense sense makes
and find ourselves happy just to see
another open-handed dawn after all.
In two thousand years will anyone

have managed to survive the non-
sense under which most governments
and love behave? I would not be
called a pessimist I think were I

to doubt it. But who am I? You
are the wise one here and I am
being as bad as your worst examples.
Maybe humans can't be taught—

or not enough of them at any
rate? Now there's a sad thought
that would take all the moving
hope out of your sails! We shall see.

I, however, will swallow all your
words into my heart, dear friend,
and reckon up my riches and against
my ornery nature surrender to reason.

[Plutarch addressed his essay
"On Peace of Mind" to Paccius,
a noble friend living in Rome.]

Sentiment for a City

There are so many poems lifted
from the streets of strange exotic cities;
I would feel a fool here
to try and pull some stubborn lyric
from the asphalt
or sound some sweet melody
from the suburban air.
I am not blind, nor is there a
seashore near to waft heroic
tales to my ear.
This is my city; the same old worn paths,
and shortcuts across the neighbors' lawns.
The plain, the practical path
to the store, the school and back.
Yet, as in Paris, I have seen
a certain sheen of sunlight falling
through the leaves that caused
my heart to lift and shimmer like
a flock of surprised wild birds.
And, as in New York, I have seen
the rainbow of peoples,
bright canvasses of life along the streets
waiting to be admired.
And, as is possible in London, there
is love here; found and won, and lost here.
This is but a place, occupied by people;
bullies and mothers, enemies and lovers,
nestled in a particular space
under the wings of the stars.

Sirius, Andromeda, Betelgeuse

This morning
the city slipped its mooring
and seemed poised
in the instance of escape
exhaust rumbling at each
buildings' base
like rocket towers
ready to flee at once
from earth
from lack of luck
from fear.
People scrambling everywhere
to take their seats
and take their chances
on some far heavens' star
away from what must be
the hugest yet of all
human disaster.

And then the morning wind
came in
and with logic on its breath
blew away the fog
and everyone rather than
on their way to an intergalactic
adventure were
on their way as every day
to work. And I was strapped
as committed as my watch is
to my wrist
as I have always
and will ever be.

Schadenfreude

I hope your grief is deep, raw—and not too brief—
aching like rotten teeth in the maw of your heart.
I hope humiliation chases you all throughout
the remainder of your too-short life, and you
cower cowed in the corner in righteous fright.

I need you to die soon, some way particularly
harsh: abscesses, cancers, seizures, and catheters.
Needles stuck everywhere—even in your eyes.
Oh, the very thought thrills and delights me, as I
want to waltz on your grave. I want to howl, loud,

enthralled over your buried body and jig and
fling on the fresh six feet of soil where under-
neath, your dismal carcass decays and putrefies.
Soon—but not right away. I want to hear first how
your loves left you, how you were turned away.

I want the descriptive details of your misery, your
full rank story, which awards you did not win, how
people squealed with laughter behind your back,
how you fell for this and how you fell for that,
which failures you felt most keenly, how the good

things soured, how all your plans went awry, what
a mess you made of things—your life—how broke
you were at the end. How finally even your family
couldn't stand you, how you were left without a
friend. I want to know how all the good deeds

you did were punished, and when you were bad
how it came back to pursue you and that when
you were sad that no one was there to care or
comfort you or offer a helping hand. I want to
be aware of how jealousy consumed you and how

envy chewed on you and how deeply you were left unsatisfied. I want to know that ages, long ago, the Principalities enrolled you on the road to Hell—how you were overwhelmingly condemned—because then I'll know, when I go, I'll have a companion in the end.

Inundation

Insane nature had in mind a rampaging ride.
Rain for weeks had soaked all the countryside,
the irate river welled, roiled, deep and wide.

Slowly at first it crept threatening up the bank
clawing its soiled fingers finally above the rank
of the highest yet muddy mark on the flank

of the bridge pillar that measures the height
of the floodtide. Then it rushed to accelerate
over and through the sandbags it ravenous ate

and spilled like spreading fingers onto the pike
disobeying the signs saying "Yield," "No Right
Turn," "Slow Children Playing," and as you might

expect, it paid least of all no attention to "Stop."
Like children freed from school it sprang, no, not
children, more like escaping convicts it sought

first, the lowly ditch and gutter, then more brave
it lifted its head and slid across the streets snake-
like and crawled on the sidewalk, in surging wave

after wave, joined by its accomplice, the endless rain
it slithered across the grass. Not content to remain
outdoors it broke and entered, chain or no chain,

lock or no lock, shoved belongings out the doors
and windows, vandalized, robbed, took from stores
and deposited its slimy, silty feces on all the floors.

Not content to violate the living, it dug its blind head
down into the saturated ground to spade at the dead.
And with sucking sounds through the secluded bed

it lifted, a second set of pallbearers, onto its shoulders
all the coffins it could carry: babies, workers, mothers,
laden with goods: sofas, albums, beds, letters—looters

with no discrimination, it had to flee. Fast as it came
but juggling merrily its ill-gotten and its rotting gain
in the weakening rain, it eddied its way back again

to the river's torrent, as swollen now with debris as water
and roiled into the rush, splashing its waves with pleasure
gleeful at all its sodden, stolen, broken, worthless treasure.

Two Impromptus and a Scherzo

Turning

Keep the tree turned toward the window.
What sun there is will find it
patiently waiting, leaves lifting.
Such a simple, caring thing, the turning
of a tree toward light. Another
domesticated being sharing the air
here, in the room where I write
some lines to friends, to what family
I have left, to editors or creditors about
a misspelling or mistake somewhere.
Always the two of us needing a turn,
a little light, some time to grow.

Unraveling

Sliding into sleep
each idea glides by
like a lighted gondola
in the dark, each gondolier
more handsome than the one before
until the one arrives we are waiting for
to take us deep into Venèzia.

On Going On
(for L.G., DDS)

This, then, is my concession
to continuance—
as I seem to have given in
to still more time—
to sit here and let him drill
and fill
and carve his mark
on these: my little
marble tombstones of teeth.

October 6, 19Never-you-mind

I am a Libra baby.
Libra, baby.
I am on the one hand,
but then on the other
weighing my way
through my unbalanced
days, feigning to all who
do not know me that I
know what I'm doing,
but, to be fair, I don't
have the foggiest notion.

It would be refreshing
to act with a semblance
of certitude in these
confusing things I must
every day decide, but
I can always see the
other damn side, so
I must stop to consider,
blocked by broad
shoulders of indecision.

I did not ask for this
to be my birth day,
better to have been
born a bold Leo or
even perhaps a sanguine
Sagittarius than this
but-both-sides vacillating
thing laying here trying to
decide whether or not I
should, on my birthday,
get the hell out of bed.

Somewhere Between
(for DBW)

I lead a hidden life, love—like
sheet lightning it licks, flickers,
and gleams there at that soft
edge between sleep and dreams.

And there you can wear any wild
thing you like, love, and you can
sing in all the colors and tongues
that you defiantly conceive of...

It began when last we met, then
scattered, and flamed to life again
when we happened on ourselves
anew, afterward, and all I can do

in that light, in that seam, in that other
hidden life I lead, love, is wait for the
shimmering like heat lightning some-
where between sleep and dreams.

Beggars Could Ride

"The world is everything that happens to be true."
— John Hollander

You would undoubtedly rather not be here.
You would rather be in Hollywood blessed
with an unforgettable face and no real fear

about money if you were genuinely pressed
to confess? I thought so. Full of good cheer
and such bonhomie, I would have guessed—

or out among a sparkling, lovely, rich group
of friends some spring night in New York,
having danced so fine that the whole troupe

backstage felt they had to let out a whoop—
and now you're out to dine, by the park,
arm-in-arm, with wit and charm, a sloop

sailing up Fifth, designer flags on parade.
(O God, I'd rather be there too, it's true.
What enormous schemes I fondly laid.)

The world is simply everything in shade,
in sun, inside or out, everything that you
know is true, and not as you had prayed.

Pointless Secrets

"Lying, the telling of beautiful untrue
things,is the proper aim of Art."
— Oscar Wilde

The truth is much too banal, cruel—
so to our will we paper over our past
and line the walls of our present
with fantasy, and taking those who
were not with us then, we bring them
by to admire our now seamless now.

The art of lying is not to be dissed.
It could, it would have been that way
but for this or that—and far more
interesting for it. Until we reach that
mirror on the wall we can almost
believe it went that way ourselves.

The others will see only their own
reflection in it though, so we keep
our pointless secrets safe and fit
for yet another fooled tomorrow.

In Too Many Ways

Allow me to attempt
to assemble you here—
perhaps in a manner
that may say what you
might have me say—
and in that way, we
could be friends?

All of my words are herein
at your disposal, and I would
have you guide me, as no
one knows you better than
you do, and how could it
hurt to be honest just this
once (as it will only pass
between us two)?

I could be kind of course
or I could lie—which
would you have it be?
But I can't crawl into
your skull and shake the
truths loose—that's not
for me to do. I'm counting
on you to tell me what
shape this takes. The pen
is yours—talk to me and
I'll take it down—and I'll
try to keep my comments
to myself.

I'm not surprised. Of course
it breaks my heart to hear it.
Who wouldn't be moved?
I might suggest that it could

be something you would not
want known—a lot of people
might not understand, after all.
This kind of enlightenment is
beyond the ability to forgive
among too many, I'm afraid.

I must say that I suspected it
though—we are alike in too,
too many ways.

On Reflection

This page is a reflection.
Depending on my mood
I could mirror your face
in all manner of light.

I can, if I wish,
put a scar right
    here
and no matter how you
turned the page
the scar would remain, or
I could make one go away
simply by saying the previous
line was a lie (even if,
as we know,
it is not so).

This mirror has unusual facets.
It can be as immediate
as the word your eyes move to
    now
or I can take you back
to the face of your childhood
(if you have the courage)
and see your speckled nose,
the horrible cow-licked hair and that
furtive, frightened look
in your eyes your parents
never noticed.

I can age you day by day
and together we can see
the skin dry and wrinkle,
sag, bag about the eyes,
watch the hair gray and fall

like human leaves and
sprinkle liver spots
onto the back of your bony hand.

I could take you beyond death
to see if your hair and fingernails
did continue to grow and how,
when the soul seeps from
the rimpled brow,
the eyes glaze and prune and dwindle
back into the shriveling brain
and how that face soon resembles
all the other skulls
more or less toothless.

But there's no need to go that far today.
Today we reflect a little hospitality
and send you on your way with
both of us knowing that now
it has been seen and shown here,
so shall you always remain.

That Someone There

Again, that someone there
in the mirror, slumming,
follows up on his promise
to meet me here faithfully
each morning in exchange
for his freedom when I
do not need him.

He never speaks unless
spoken to and only says
those things I already know.
When he leaves, he doesn't
tell me his destinations nor
when he reappears does he
tell me where he's been.

I only know that beyond
the reflection behind me
he exits into a world that
has no snow, no living to
make, and no one to
answer to. It has not
stopped his aging, though,
sadly he has time to go
through as all of us must do,
I would save him from that
if I could, but time is as
much a necessity to his
species as it is to mine.

He meets me and passes
no judgment anymore—
we are far beyond that in
our tortured relationship—
and when dismissed, he

visits a place far different
from that which waits dully
outside my door. It is, per-
haps, to an unfallen Eden,
a young lover, the coast of
Spain—or to speak with
luminaries, walk through
Paris streets, or to meals
with friends I will never meet.

I envy him—not for his looks of
course which are unfortunately
fading and weren't much to
begin with, but because he goes
where they don't matter and
never have, where meadows
bloom in the laps of Matterhorns,
where limousines whisk him
safe from place to place, where
music continues still from those
composers who have stepped
beyond this planet where
I scuff my shoes.

This is what I have promised
him in return: I will not ask
where he has been, and he
will leave me to my imagining.

Depending on the Time of Day

"I am coming to think now that
all I have loved are shadows."
— John Heath-Stubbs

Depending on the time of day,
the shade takes its own way
behind me, or hurries ahead,
or strides alongside as though
it might be my lover or at least
a friend. But it's nothing more
than my one-sided conversation
that keeps me company. Even
under the trees where I seek to
shake my dark comrade, it stays—
shadowed in the shade of the
penumbra where I tread.

From Ra to nuclear fire-ball,
neither Sovereign nor slave
can escape the phantoms that
the daylight wreaths wraith-like
at our feet—unless gone still in
sharp silhouette, no one would
know it was you—not like finger-
prints or DNA, it could, if moving,
never give you away.

In dinner candlelight though,
it is those shadows played
on the planes of your face
that hold sway—they make
a memory and, with age,
all that stay.

In a line-up of those accused,
bright lights hide them away.

Though I am a guilty one as well,
I look anyway, drop all charges
and set you free. Leaving, all
I finally have comes with me,
behind, alongside, in front
of me under the passing
streetlights into the night,
toward sleep, with sweet
shadows beneath me.

Plenty of Time

There's plenty of time, we tell ourselves,
we always say, when stepping out into
another beleaguered day, to begin again,
to fight another battle at a better time.
Yet hour is swallowed by ensuing hour
never to be seen again, as 8 o'clock today
disappears forever and 8 o'clock tomorrow
is a different animal altogether even though
they share the same name and repeat their
character on whichever device we choose
to track their presence and their passing.

There's never enough time, Time will tell
us in return if we listen: we go on, second
succumbing to second, minutes in legions
murdering the hours as the Present dies
quietly in the arms of the Past taking some
of us with them, but we will go on saying
there's plenty of time, meaning more than
enough, a sufficient amount, to do what we
intend to do, or mean to do, or hope to do,
as 8 o'clock is scythed by the hands of 9.

Silent/Listen

I really shouldn't be saying anything,
I ought to be listening instead.
"Silent" and "listen" use the same
letters, which should tell me
something, but I feel somehow
compelled to fill the vacant air
with my meanderings, connecting
yet one more word with another
blocking the air as though out of
fear I were building a wall to keep
others out or myself within.

(The only thing that should be allowed
to take over the quiescence of solitary
hours without permission is music;
words need to step back then and
bow to its superior nobility and keep
still, as melody always has something
profound to say that words will never
be able to fathom, no matter how many
we may try to marshal against it.)

Yes, so I ought to be listening, ought
to be holding my bustling, seemingly
tireless tongue, and let others or even
stillness have its say. I am too fond of
my foolish prattling at the end of the
day, too proud of my loud assessment
of too many issues, too sympathetic
to my ceaseless matters of opinion and
too bewitched by my impudent babbling...

I'm sorry, I'm sorry, what did you say?

Finalities
(for Kenneth Fenwick
on the death of his father)

1.

There is in the air, finalities—if restless—
These new days have brought new deaths,
and one lone one here.

And the air of October, this autumn, this fall,
draws folds of red and gold down to cover all,
down from the mountains,

as if to comfort the beginning of the end
of the year. Restless air that will not suspend
its duties for a day,

and snaps out leaves as would an aide,
unmindful of what or who has gone ahead,
flaps over the bed

a clean, fresh, white sheet that billows down
like the snow that will follow soon and slow.
The seasons flow.

2.

And so, old man, Poppy, this is what has brought us to truce:
this finality, this last day, and all I have to give you is my voice.
They are just words, entangled in a half-century of memory,
and once unfurled they disappear into the restless air so easily

there will be nothing left to see what has been said: transparent
words. If they had color perhaps some would linger here evanescent
for a moment, to slant some light into the darkness of our sorrow,
but we are human, mortal, we will go without into tomorrow.

All of us gathered here know something dissimilar about you.
Though my flesh was spun of your flesh, I was not easy to love
nor could I sometimes find my way to give your devil his due.

All our lives are complicated, messy, fissured in many ways—
we clash, we generate mistakes, we fail to say "I love you,"
but like words in restless air, you are entangled in our days.

Burying Aunt Bev

Another mother's coffin
stirred with flowers into
the soil.
Grandmother, grandfather,
mother and brother scattered
family plot-less across
the vast green expanse
of Crown Hill.

There is that
disappearance
and the anger that comes from never
any words in this language
or any other
louder or wiser
to explain or drown out
the sound of one heartbeat
less.

Death scythes my pale words
into a bouquet that you can
see through right into day,
my last words, frail and inadequate
to the interred scintillance she was
are no longer in the air.

And we drive away and leave
her settled there, for the tilling
workers who linger, who seal
over the scarred soil with
sod, and fill the fast-healed
air with baseball scores
and unrelated,
unrelated
conversation.

Wystan: A Requiem
September 29, 1973

We do not know nor do we much
care what the weather was that day,
what we do know was that you died
alone 25 miles away from your final
home in a hotel room, far from York
and New York of an enlarged heart.

Was it a cloudless night like this,
was it a tiresome day, after all? And
did your spirit soar under the 18th-
century stars of a baroque sky in
Vienna, unshocked by the bawdy
thoughts of your 17-year-old self?

Most of us are unready to die, did
you know it was the last night to
consider that scattered sprinkle
of stars? What last words did you
leave them with, did you have too
much to drink again do you think?

When you went to lay your soon-to-
be sleeping head on your solo pillow,
under your notorious layers of heavy
blankets you were not aware you
would awaken to find your rumpled,
stained, and disheveled self wearing

well-worn slippers walking out that
evening into an applauding Universe.

Until Then, Then

We dropped Mother off
near the old neighborhood in '76
and my sister some years later
in Nepal.

There was nowhere else to go
but forward for us, holding on, no
traveling back to say hello, no *you forgot this*,
no last kiss—

we had to go. Time waits for none
of us, because Time can't care.
Time has its schedule until we lie down,
let it go,

carrying our friends and careening.

Elegy
(for my father: 1924-2019)

What is this thing called dying? One day
you're doing, the next day you're done.
The bells tolling day in, day out, ringing
out only the toll, counting, never their
names, just the numbers, one by one.

The widow insisted on no words though
the dead don't know. Sad, that was all I
had, but no one showed to the viewing
anyway, old as he was, his friends gone
on ahead alone as well, as we all will do.

The days afterward drone, murmuring
on; Emily's sainted hour of lead is gray
and weighs on into the week ahead and
taints even the summer air and sun with
shade none involved can seem to shake.

Time taps impatiently on our shoulder,
tells us to move on, that was yesterday;
and tomorrow drags us beyond with its
long leash of this and that to do, and has
neither patience nor sufferance for Now.

What choice do we have? None. Forward
is the only door, the dirt is already drying,
settled, packed, smoothed, for seeding in
the spring; and so we go, out of weeping
into needing to breathe. That is how it is
done.

Present in Time Future
(for Rémy Lestienne)

Although we have devised clocks
that go counter-clockwise (a joke),
still that time goes forward backward,
the clicking of each second seen to be
indicating that the day might go down in
the East, that the wrinkles might smooth
out as the day diminishes (we wish!).
It's the same with a stopped clock, dead
(right twice a day), still time goes ahead
going ahead, even though those out-
stretched hands are seen to be embracing
a perennial present.

Although it is life itself that allows time
to be—or vice-versa—the ones we miss
will never resurrect on their way to the
womb, the diseases will never be returned
to whence they came, the fallen rain will
never revert the same way to the sky nor
tears to the eyes nor love, once it is gone,
will ever reinhabit the heart. Yet memory,
against all the force and flow of nature
pushes the past into the present and
the future falls easily back through the
barriers of forward and awes us here,
looking up the steep dark sides of the well
to where the starlight shines over now.

Survive, Survive
(for J.T. Fraser)

This species has need for six things to survive:
to eat, to drink, to sleep, to dream, to breathe,
and to move forward, only forward through time.

We well know how to handle the first easier five,
we have a physical hand in them, we easily weave
them in and through our days combining fine

designs into the tapestry—mostly. We will notice
where we've made our errors but can't turn back
to repair or correct them—no reweaving allowed,

because to pause to fix even the most woeful stitch
dropped, missed, would stop the clock, would block
the sixth thing, time, as it unspindles and has flowed

from first remembered moment until today, until
now, this instant patched into retention, and done,
with only the urgency, the headlong drive to carry on.

It is substance. We can't see it, taste it, touch its twill,
we can only know it has been, gone, spun, badly sewn
or brilliantly so—what's done, done. In creped linen
or unraveling gunny: none perfect, none forgiven.

Abiding

"If you find a penny,
put it into your left shoe
and make a wish."
— *Lula Bales*

Just to make it there,
to make it there is all I ask.
Whether it is by some admirable
triumph of will
or as foolish as wishing
on a penny found
face up on the asphalt
and put with some balancing
into my left shoe, I want
to follow through.

I can't help but hope—
because I am a fool—
I can't do anything but believe
that it will all be worthwhile,
this listening to the never-ending
words, this catching them
in my hand, this setting them alight
to see if they will
push the shadows back
at least as far
as the corners
of this room.

Visiting my Father

Colorado is unreal
from the back seat
of a Cadillac and when
you have been
so very long away.

Remember the '54 Pontiac?
floored to hit the top
of the pass and
    wallowing
  down
around the curves before
they put our tax dollars to work
knocking down the hissing S signs?

And then there was water
we could drink there—
at the top, spilling from
hidden springs—cold enough
to make your fillings ring while
the car caught its elephantine breath?

There where the water on the one side
went west
and on the other, east?

In autumn daylight, the golden coins of aspen
hurt our eyes. At night
our breath echoed the Milky Way
in long white sighs across the sky.

Father's Day
That Tough Protective Husk

The sharp bright axe of age
has finally hewn its way through
that tough protective husk
of my father's memory.

With no one left to share
it with, he separates
the shiny seeds that
shaped his life and

spreads them out like
gems, like vari-colored
jewels, like diamonds,
but not neglecting the dull stones

that ground him to a smoother
sheen that took the rougher
edges off that polished him
to a singular undying shine.

Suzy Had a Farm
(for Suzy Jacobson)

Suzy had a farm.
Plum Creek ran through it.
When I was young,
when the cousins were young
(and now I know that
the uncles and aunts
and my mother and father
were young then too),
old Suzy—her face
a landscape of dry
creek beds, her hair
a gray explosion in a bun,
a mouth full of
big yellow bones defining
her smile—would tractor
a clearing under the cottonwoods
and the poor lot of us would Sunday picnic there.

Fried chicken, deviled eggs,
fresh corn from Suzy's fields we would be
forced to shuck
boiled in a big pot, potato salads, iced pop;
gooseberry, rhubarb, and cherry pies;
sneaking sips from uncles' beers (while
my father pretended not to see my cousins
sip his) and all us naked kids
in the creek shrieking and chasing craw-dads
and racing sticks. The grandmas and grandpas
and a fragile, sweet old great-grandma queen,
would sit and tell the same old stories they told
each other the last time and drowse
in the shade while softball went on
in the meadow and Suzy taught
some of us how to dowse.

During the Depression, when her husband died,
grandpa was her closest neighbor and
was always there to help and we became
then part of her inheritance.
She laughed all the time.
When we cut ourselves, she painted
the wounds with kerosene.
She always looked us straight in the face
and wore blue overalls that matched her eyes that
Mom would say could stand up by themselves.
That was before the divorces and the deaths,
when Suzy was the mother of us all
and Eden was her farm.

The Extras Remaining

Weariness
and a cramp in my lower back
from lifting trays
from leaning over a table
to hear above the din
their never-ending orders.

It's being stuck in a small
dull play doing a bit part
for little pay.
Always smiling.

Saying my name, soon forgotten,
auditioning a new pleasantness
or line to try and pry at least a grin
or please another dollar
from someone whose mind is
already satisfied about the tip.

And the evening stretches from
the outside fork in,
from first appetizer
to last dessert,
playing the tables through
attempting to determine
which demand, if delayed,
will cause the least damage.

And so it goes,
run after run,
with only the extras remaining
to serve night after night
of stars.

Puppet

Up from where my feet should be
comes my filling out with flesh,
the gloving of my being.

My coming into consciousness
makes me giddy, silly—
but laughter, after all,
is the reason, the entire
explication of my meaning.

Children don't care how small
or dumb I appear and they hand
up the child I was from an older
heart thought lost somewhere.

Le Piano Zinc Bar, Paris

I go out at night
dressed as best I can
to resemble someone's fantasy,
showing off my arms and chest,
my waist wrestled by exercise
to its narrowest, my legs
long and lean (hoping that
the face, puttied by chance,
will not be too closely seen).

Lust goes with me,
living bravely in the dark;
wise bars knowing too much light
will drive her bat-like self out
into the streets, long having learned
that alcohol's haze helps
to veil our all-too-human
flaws and ways.

Over the Piaf,
over the singing,
show tunes and lovelorn,
a few narrow words,
gingerly compared coins
are exchanged, an
evening deal struck,
and as we leave,
the billions of years of history that
needle the night in
cold and glittering spikes of light
do not ask our names.

The Morning After the
Walpurgisnacht Before
(for TRG)

The day is over, the week is done, we
lock tomorrow's threats and worries
away from now and set out to sink
our teeth into an unfolding present, one
second dropped to greet another as if
the former never mattered on our way
to the next steam-letting pleasure we
deserve for all the pressure every day
with its seeming vengeance wreaks.

We go out this dark evening, singing,
to lark, out where the devil lives in
dim lighting in one place and where
in others, phantasmagoric flashes
dart around the room while primal beats
in pulsing chords scream out themes
of debauchery we do not demur from
responding to as we bruise the floor
with dancing feet, whirling with rhythms
accelerating our heartbeat thumping
with questionable, illicit substances
purchased in a black-shadowed street.

As the night unrolls we ride like demons
around and down the drowning hours,
devouring a new sweet someone's mouth,
howling like dreamers forced to rise from
nightmare's tortures, folding yet another
into our undiscriminating arms—as love
for now is better than love never found.

When dawn arrives with the white rays
of the Sunday morning sun streaming,

we red-eyed wander our sated way home
reeling from too much of us spent sore
and depleted through the near empty
streets, and over the urban trees bells are
ringing, and the choirs cry out in longing
through the pellucid air and praising
Christ in crisp, chaste phrases.

Aging Out

Youth is lovely in the lilting lies
it tells itself. You see them not
seeing you and you know you
were the same unseeing self at
that discriminating age and why
not? Like is attracted to like in
that libidinous stage and lovely
has magic in its opening blooms.

At the gym you see the skin that
hasn't yet gone thin with all the
years that have rubbed against
it, and at the bar you see the well-
groomed heads and the eyes that
glaze over when their gaze is sent
out roaming the room set on stun.
That's the way of it with the young.

I hold them no grudge; in a way
it's good to step back away from
the roiling parade and watch the
dancers who don't know how time
will come to separate them from
the dance and let them play. And
anyway they will not see the naked
shade of me ricochet among them.

Separate Ways
(for TRG)

Sleeping—or almost—
in the sun on the beach,
my body oiled and warm,
the breeze unreeling in off the sea,

the light candling my lids
to rose petals, the long waves
a low-throated sigh and lullaby
and so why, here, in this quiet place

should this particular thought,
a jolt, ice-water, ice-pick memory
crack like an electric shock
through my almost dreaming and reverie?

I had hoped to pour at least an ocean between us.

Maybe Some Night

I once was an only,
now only an ex,
(one among many,
we could note,
but we shouldn't
keep score) yet
you slip sometimes
into my sleep and
set up shop as
though you had
never left and act
as though nothing
has changed. It's
strange to find you
inside my, or should
I say, our house,
moving around like
you own the place.

I can remember when
I would think ahead to
when I would be able
to turn to you and say,
Do you remember when?
and then that turned
into never because
neither of us will ever
be together again to
remember again. So,

we meet then in our
sleep, my dreams, and
behave as though we
believe it never came
to an end, and some-

times we say sweet things
and kiss again and maybe
some night I will remember
and turn to you or you to
me and one of us will say,
Do you remember when?

Dark before Dawn

I woke to the shudder of dreams
about spiders (my grandmother
would call that good luck) and
landed damp in the dark before dawn.

Another long night to set
as companion against the short days.
Another twenty-four hours bitten off
by the black-jawed clock.

Like the sighs of the sea,
the sounds of traffic rise and
fall into the ears of
early morning.

It will be another stormy day
steaming toward evening.

Now, however, for the moment
it is safe—
standing in this kitchen
the purchased hours have bought,

listening to the coffee pot
chug its blood from clear
to brown, waiting for the only other
boy alive

before the light
to bicycle by and throw
this mornings' meat of history
at my door.

And still the sun has not risen
with its rose of optimism, nor

has the dry face of the moon
fallen to farther dark horizons.

The heavens are suspended
somewhere between the hands
of yesterday and today and
promises are neither held up

nor withdrawn. There is a peace
between us now—
between being and dawn.

Seasons

Winter is about to haul
her hard white body
over here. The trees
are prickly with their
dismemberment, their brownish
bones pick in the wind
at a graying sky.

There are reasons for all
of it—just as the first burst of
snow sounds the downbeat
beyond the 4/4 cadence
that makes the weather here
so unrelentingly reliable.

Success has seasons,
plots do, life does,
and that which we choose
to call love, among other things.

Weather Whether

Out front the tree is spattered
with small white explosions
of blossoms; the wasps are
giddy with nectar-glee.

The world has curved far over
the year into another summer,
and the sun sprawls lazy, torrid,
naked, luxuriantly across the sky.

I wisely stay within with ice
recalling sweltering climate in
days gone by, when I was
unfazed by heat on asphalt

streets, and interrupted ditches
with my dancing feet. That,
and wondering whether I have
the wherewithal to weather even

one more short season into winter.

Bouquet Recherché

I should know the names of plants
and flowers, almost every fine poet
worth their MFA does. They trellis
their lines with their proper names,
evoking hue and perfume to all
who know their biological genera.
(It was never anything I was disposed
to learn—a lot like algebra—out
of my ability and realm of interest,
should I be embarrassed to confess?)

I look of course, commending their
manifold shapes and complex scents
to myself, but city-bred and respecting
their privacy, I never make so bold as
to ask their cognomen any more than
I would go up to a handsome human
face and say *My, what's your lineage?*
You are so very lovely and you smell
quite nice. That would be rude and
an invasion of personal space.

Oh, I know daisies and roses, sun-
flowers, baby's breath, carnations
and the like—same as I know who
the Windsors, Clintons, Bushes (the
murdering kind), and Barrymores
are, but beyond the more famous,
I generally intend not to intrude.

You're more likely to find something
else here I'm afraid: a basketful of
adverbs, perhaps, a word so rare
it sends you grumbling, disgruntled

to the dictionary, or an off-putting
British spelling (which at the time
seemed appropriate), the scent of
fried flesh, a reference to a deservedly
long-forgotten minor god who tickled
my fancy from I don't remember where.
That's about as natural and botanical
as it gets around here.

As close as I come to the usual florae
is esteeming that dogged and obstinate
weed that shoves a disheveled head
above the asphalt or the one that
seems to be able to feed off oil-spills
in an alley in a dark and somewhat
seedy neighborhood. That untended
grit and spit, that indomitable will
among the more ugly among us is
admirably and wonderfully made.

The world would be a bitter and
dour place without the flowers yes,
I accept. We need the lilies' funereal
perfume, the purpled song of the choir
wisteria, the nobility of the rose, but
if like me, you find yourself roaming
in reality, out along the ditch and
gutter, out among the vacant lots
or untidy fields, find a second to
spare for the spirit that defies the
disdain of the ordered gardener and
those who advocate for compliance
and tame, who make what they will
of their seasonal life and rise and
rise again.

Scenting Fall

Afraid to look down
because it may be so far—
or it may not—
and who knows what is
waiting under those
leafy, crackling shadows
below? I'm not sure
I want to find out yet
(just because it's arrested
doesn't mean it's not a fall
you know), although it requires
no effort, no effort at all
in letting go.

At thirty-two feet
per second, per second
(is that it? Gravity
at the speed of time?)
stopped long enough
by white and anxious-knuckled
fingertips, feet flailing,
to fit in a few panicked wonderings,
scenting Fall.

Looking up I see that the nut is
not far from the tree metaphorically
speaking and knowing all the
while that though I never asked
to go up, I must in good conscience
and in good time, come down to root,
to reality, and to earth.

Sufficient Light to See

We are going to put everything in order—
even these synapses that solder themselves
together and like street lamps illuminate
the way in or out of the city all the way
to an as yet undeveloped pasture.

There is no one light, bright or single sun here,
only the occasional star and the look
back or forward to what the lamp beam
behind or ahead illuminates up the hill
or down or around the corner.

The whole landscape will have to wait
for a fire, a comet, or a nova to overarch
the sky with sufficient light to see.
Until then, string another feeble lantern
at the end of the road and throw a shadow

as far as you can.

On the Other Hand...

"I begin to speak only when I'm certain
what I'll say isn't better left unsaid."
– Cato the Younger

There's no need to prod trouble,
it will rise and bite you anyway.
No need to rail against the winter
wind, it will stab at you and stab
again. No need to long for wealth,
it will not visit you no matter how
many invitations you send.

There's no need to fancy after
fame, it has looked you over and
found you wanting. No need to
pray, the rules of the Universe
have been written and No One
will break them for you even if
you spend all your allotted years
weeping down on your knees.

There's no need to look for some-
one to love, they will find you first,
then leave. No need to cry when
they have left—it was for the best.
No need to apologize for your feelings,
no one else will know what you mean.
No need to ask for forgiveness, that
which is done has been achieved.

There is no need to look in the mirror,
no face you recognize will be there.
No need to check the footnotes of
history, they will tell you nothing you
don't already know. No need to speak
of the unspeakable, it has all been

said with eloquence elsewhere. No
need to walk with me all the way—
I think I know where to go from here.

Some Morning

I will wake up
some strafed morning,
in some sodden spring,
in some sizzling summer,
in some autumn full
of the leaves of regret,
or on a white winter morning
when the world is frozen
gaunt with anguish and
despair and say
I have gone far enough.

I will never unleash
the ferocity of an orchestra
on my favorite Allegro
molto vivace and feel
its fury consume the air.
I will never catch
the dying ballerina
as she falls swooning
into the muscular care
of my loving arms.
I will never carve a
chimera out of marble
or make a brushstroke
to fascinate you for hours.

But some morning, perhaps
with tenderness, you will
hold this and know that
had I been better, dreamed
larger, but not loved you
less, all of this and more
would have been yours
before I said
I have gone far enough.

On Losing

If we are astute—or just
worn out from being
world-weary—we have
wisely given up believing
that gods or goddesses
(our friend Emily slyly
addressed It as an
Eclipse) will send us
those things we fervently
long for.

It is left instead to Lady
Luck, or Dame Fortune,
or to be correct and un-
gendered about it, the
Wheel, to deliver our
secret desires to us—
but unfortunately, with
those, whichever you
choose, you either lose
or win because the
very definition of it is
that it is, at best, a
crapshoot.

It would be nice, God knows,
if there were some caring
Creature-thing somewhere
abiding in the ether who was
bothered sufficiently over
us to give a good damn about
our well-being or our sorrows
(and if there should be, at this
point, It could only be, to be
kind, characterized as some-

thing consisting of Supreme
Indifference)—just some gentle
Divine to send out a kind word
to the Universe to bend its
wayward will to our wanting
ways?

What we have is what we've
already got with unruly luck.
And still—still and all—we
stumble out into the slant
of that early morning sun
squinting at the hours ahead
and betting, against all the
other hapless days we've
ditched to get this far, that
this one is it, and that it will
somehow magic itself into
something somewhat more
otherworldly, or in some
notable, noticeable measure,
more kind.

The Upper Hand

I have been out waltzing with Lady Luck;
wise always to the melody, prima ballerina,
she outdoes me and my stumbling steps
attempting to keep up are clumsy, comical.

There at the corner, turning, she saved me
and I live to drive another day, and there
the knife slips and slides away sideways,
she knew it was after my dumb pink thumb.

I drag her along to play the lottery, but to
tease in her circumspect way, she stays
laughingly noncommittal and can only say,
We'll see, we'll see and winks knowingly.

She knows not that I can't live without her,
but that I won't; so she has the upper hand.
And I know someday she will desert me, but
I go on and love her as long, as hard as I can.

Ars longa

There.
Not enough to warrant
a footnote in your page
of days perhaps, but there,
recognized or remembered—
likely not—
though to fool and flatter
myself I like to think so...

Your days unroll in a
seemingly endless melody
skittering from strings to
woodwinds to brass
and back unfolding...
And there among the
orchestration some small
trilling notes in a section
written in a minor key.

Painted over perhaps
in a patch that to your
eye called for a more
celestial hue?
But there, hidden
in the canvas if you look,
I am there, there
inside of you.

Plusses and Minuses

So where do you go from here?
All our choices are born from one
we had no voice in. What have you
piled up behind you—which was
the best and which the worst and
where do you go from there, then?

You packed up the things you had
worth saving and set off again into
yet a new uncertainty as none of us
can see what's up the street, around
the corner, down the block, over that
far too high a hill ahead with the sun
in our eyes, the fitful wind in our face.

We can calculate with what we've got:
this worked before but not that, won't
make that mistake again, we tell our
tutored selves, shaking our educated
head, and let's not even think about
that mess we made (though it wasn't
all that bad, if we discard the carcass,
and ignore the embarrassment and the
shame and the trauma it caused us).

If you add up your guesses, take the
plusses and minuses, multiply by
the best and the worst experiences
and divide by the degree of bravery
you can muster, you can reckon your
way to something maybe resembling
a decision, or, at best, a rationalization
for what you ultimately choose to do.

We can't go back, much as we might

want to, that's all ossified; we can't
stand still, no sane person would say
that this is the place to be. Sideways
doesn't dissolve the fog in front of us,
so shoulder your bags, say goodbye
to the moment, and though we were
given no voice in that original choice,
Onward, comrades—it can't be much
worse.

Meditation in the Color of C

There are so many things
I give up to speak to you this
way—the sound of course,
and the color. If I could render
"Spring" in hues of green
or "Autumn" in contrasting
characters of gold and red—
would that enhance the meaning
or be too much? I can't modulate
the nuance by moving from C
to B-flat minor here either.

But I go on, nonetheless, singing
(or croaking, rather) my way
through my thoughts as even
the chiming of rhyming is no
longer allowed. (I feel compelled
though to sneaking it in
when no one is looking.)
Still, it would be fun to impasto
"lust" in a reddish-rust (there, you
caught me!) or "serenity" in varying
gradations of violet and gray.

Narratives, like those for children
would be enlivened by a bit of
crimson illustration, the cardinal
in the bare winter tree, the sherry left
at the bottom of a guest's glass. The
waltz at the ball in Eugene Onegin
can be done: *One*, two, three, *One*,
two, three—imagine the melody.

I can only give you some simple
black on white, *black* on white,

or point your nose toward the memory
of a rose, I suppose—but if I want
to take you all the way there with me,
you have to join me as co-conspirator,
painting the roses red for the Queen,
or watching for pink petals on a wet
black bough at a station of the Metro.

I want you to surrender to me—
I may or may not love you, but
it is necessary for you to believe
that I do so you can look into my
eyes and see your unforgettable
face reflected there as I do, so you
will fall into us at this moment
in a chorus of color and in an
incandescence of song.

Farewell

Fare well.
Old-fashioned phrase,
but what better way
to say Goodbye than
to wish your friends or
family that they go into
a future where you
cannot be or see what
fortune has in store
for them?

Wishing them well—
a kind thought thrown
like a coin into a wishing
well, but not for our own
profit. We should bring it
back again and hand it out
at the end of each meeting
to last until the next happy
greeting when we encounter
them on our way through
our own unfolding folders
of days.

There are so many who
have walked away from
my daily life I don't ever
expect to see again, some
still living, fortunately,
but sadly I can't call up
what last I said to any
loving one of them. Had
I been more cognizant of
how ways turn into ways,
I wish I would have had

burrowed that phrase more
deeply into my every day
vocabulary and had said,
dear friend,
my love,
above all,
fare well.

Closer

Look at it and all you'll see, hung on a white line,
is black ribbons against a white sky. Meaning?
Nothing. Nothing unless you get close. The fine
weave of these tatters matter, mean something,

must mean something. They are worn but not
scraps to be discarded or they wouldn't be hung
with such care. Someone wanted you to stop,
someone wanted you to get closer. Someone.

But you can pass on by—many have, many will.
You have no obligation to pause and consider,
no armed authority will force you to a stand-still,
there's been no ruling passed in any legislature,

no moral law demanding that you must delay or
linger there. It cannot not make you any more
wise, nor much more beautiful; you can ignore
it completely if you wish, there's not much store

taken in it anymore, and at the end, when death
wrestles you to bed, it will not even be known
whether you had stopped here to take a breath—
you only would have been a little less alone.

End Credits

I was in the book business for over thirty years. One thing I know is that a book is never one person, it's a passel of them. When everyone's jostling to get out of the movie house, the end credits are rolling. There never would have been a movie without all of them. Out of respect, I never leave until all the names have appeared on the screen. Hopefully you'll give these important names a moment or two here?

There would have been no book without Bruce Joshua Miller, long-time colleague in that book business, who insisted I put a manuscript together, I told him he was bats, he told me do it anyway and he would try to find them a home, and much to my astonishment he did. One more time, and may it resonate in every copy printed, "Thank you, Bruce. You embody what every mensch aspires to be."

The late William ("Wild Bill") Tillson, poet, professor, mentor, and tough guy, put me hard through my paces, wrote "Good/poets make good critics," in his poetry volume *Walden Invaded*, in which he inscribed when I won my first (and only) award, "To David Perkins, the best student of poetry, and the best critic..." and therefore made me think maybe.

Kathleen Cain, poet, naturalist, *il miglior fabbro*, was not only midwife to some of these, she blew life into many I did not think could survive. She overturned her life for months so my cat and I would have a place to eat, to sleep, to recover, to dream. If you don't believe in Queen Mab—or munificence—or magic, you must meet her and read her poems.

Jay Miller, artist, illustrator, decadence survivor, said "These talk to me, let me show you what I see," and walked out and among the lines and saw whole new vistas and perspectives and gifted those to me.

The editors of *Christopher Street Magazine, The Chariton Review, Grasshopper, The Bloomsbury Review, When the Bluebird Sings, High Plains Literary Review, Sága* and others, all venues now gone, sacrificed on the Internet's altar of expediency—I will never forget the pleasure and the excitement of seeing print on paper, nor the kindness of your belief in me. To Lola Morgan, who awarded First Place to "I Should Have No Doubts" for the Ann Woodbury Hafen Award. And of course resplendent thanks to Steve Semken and the good offices of Ice Cube Press who have been kind enough to give these a final resting place.

So many more—you know what you did, what it meant, and why you are here; names only (but hints!), out of respect for privacy, secrecy, reasons either of culpability or just too sweet and intimate to share and in no particular order: because "...there, hidden/in the canvas if you look,/I am there, there/inside of you:"

The aforementioned Daysun Perkins, Perfection; Larry Perkins, Dad, who loved me anyway; Suzanne Jacox, dwelling in the Always Good; Laurence DiPaolo, *Nessun Dorma!* and Norma; Kenneth Fenwick; *Speak what we feel, not what we ought to say*; Beth Ann Maliner, *To live is so startling...*; Marilyn Auer, *Books, cats, life is good*; Alexandra Roberts, *Fasten your seatbelts*; Dana Boyd, *This better be good*; Jeanne Creighton Redmond, Hearts and who Gorey was born for; Katherine Kellogg Martin, *What d'ya say, old friend?*; Patricia DiNenno Malaspina, *That's crazy!*; Dawn W. Petersen, *Dance when you're perfectly free*; Melissa Snell, Tree houses and sentient beings; Pennie Magee, *Tenho mais almas que uma*; Douglas Wayman, *What we are is an illusion*; Tom George, Kong loved getting into trouble; David Rile, Doors are to go through. And all the cats: Fuzzy Whiskers, Sable, Mother and Baby and Fritz, Reachin' and Hypsipyle, Ramses and Petya, Emily and Jessie and Mr. Petes and Bette. Finally, Michael DiNenno, *That's nice. Did you clean the litter box?* It's been a long journey, Love.

One more if I may? My lifelong avocation has been as an amateur scholar learning and writing about the life and music of Pyotr Ilyich Tchaikovsky. In him you will find every human emotion ennobled, from unfettered joy to profound sorrow filtered through his remarkable sensibilities. I have not found a single work in his canon that has failed to touch me in some visceral way. I know his flaws (and so did he), but his humanity saves him from those. If there are any melodies to be found in this book, they are his.

The Ice Cube Press began publishing in 1991 to focus on how to live with the natural world and to better understand how people can best live together in the communities they share and inhabit. Using the literary arts to explore life and experiences in the heartland of the United States we have been recognized by so many generous and well-known writers it's beyond graceful, including, but not in any way limited to: Gary Snyder, Gene Logsdon, Wes Jackson, Patricia Hampl, Greg Brown, Jim Harrison, Annie Dillard, Ken Burns, Roz Chast, Jane Hamilton, Daniel Menaker, Kathleen Norris, Janisse Ray, Craig Lesley, Alison Deming, Harriet Lerner, Richard Lynn Stegner, Richard Rhodes, Michael Pollan, David Abram, David Orr, Tom Brokaw, and Barry Lopez. We've published a number of well-known authors including: Mary Swander, Jim Heynen, Mary Pipher, Bill Holm, Connie Mutel, John T. Price, Carol Bly, Marvin Bell, Debra Marquart, Ted Kooser, Stephanie Mills, Bill McKibben, Craig Lesley, Elizabeth McCracken, Derrick Jensen, Dean Bakopoulos, Rick Bass, Linda Hogan, Pam Houston, and Paul Gruchow. Check out Ice Cube Press books on our web site, join our email list, Facebook group, or follow us on Twitter. Visit booksellers, museum shops, or any place you can find good books and support true honest to goodness independent publishing projects so you can discover why we continue striving to "hear the other side."

Ice Cube Press, LLC (Est. 1991)
North Liberty, Iowa, Midwest, USA
steve@icecubepress.com
we also twitter and facebook as surfers of the web
www.IceCubePress.com

Answering "If I May or May Not"
To Fenna Marie
with nary any doubts ever *I love you*
To Ingrid
I entirely and whole full heartedly *love you*